Customer Experience Management

Author: Brooke R. Envick

Dr.Envick.consulting

Taking Your Business to the Nex⚡Level

an affiliate of
San Antonio Business Leadership Academy - The Dynamic Leader

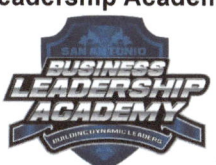

cXM

CUSTOMER EXPERIENCE MANAGEMENT

What is a Customer Experience?

A customer experience is an interaction between something related to your business and a customer followed by the perception the customer forms either consciously or subconsciously. Many things in your business blend together to create a specific experience for each customer. There may be a few or several "touch points" that occur, meaning the customer has an interaction with a few things/people or with many things/people.

CXM has become a critical differentiator in today's hyper-competitive, hyper-connected global marketplace. Your will find tangible business value in managing the customer experience effectively. Good customer experience management can:

- Strengthen brand preference through differentiated experiences.
- Boost revenue with incremental sales from existing customers and new sales from
  word of mouth.
- Improve customer loyalty (and create advocates) through valued and memorable customer interactions.
- Lower costs by reducing customer churn.

What is Customer Experience Management (CXM)?

Customer Experience Management (CXM) is a fairly straight forward and simple, yet comprehensive means of auditing your customer's entire experience. It is a process that addresses the full spectrum of their wants and needs. There are several intersecting messages, product or service features, opinions, and emotions felt along the way. You want your customers to view your business as a *value* to them, which results in being more profitable, being better aligned strategically within the market, and helping to ensure sustainability. Research suggests that businesses who offer the best customer experiences have lower customer churn and more customer referrals.

Establishing Connection & Participation

CXM means that *you take control* of how your business interacts with your customers. This is done by viewing your business and your customer entirely from the customer's perspective. This requires establishing a *connection* with your customer and getting your customers to *participate* in their experience with your business. The two most important outcomes are to build customer loyalty and generate positive word of mouth. Consider your five senses: sight, smell, touch, hearing, and taste. Then, think of ways to connect to customers and elicit their participation through one or more of their senses.

Stage 1:   **Stage 2:**   **Stage 3:**

Take Control	Outcome	Reward
Form Connections	Loyalty	Boost in Revenue
Opportunities for Participation	Referrals	Reduce Customer Churn

Economic Distinctions

Economic Distinctions				
Economic Offering	Commodities	Goods	Services	Experiences
Economy	Agrarian	Industrial	Service	Experience
Economic Function	Extract	Make	Deliver	Stage
Nature of Offering	Fungible	Tangible	Intangible	Memorable
Key Attribute	Natural	Standardized	Customized	Personal
Method of Supply	Stored in bulk	Inventoried after production	Delivered on demand	Revealed over a duration
Seller	Trader	Manufacturer	Provider	Stager
Buyer	Market	User	Client	Guest
Factors of Demand	Characteristics	Features	Benefits	Sensations

Coffee beans are a commodity that cost between $1-$2 per pound, and that translates to 1-2 cents per cup. When a manufacturer grinds the coffee beans and packages it for grocery stores, the price per cup jumps to 10-25 cents per cup (depending on brand and package size). Brewing the coffee grinds for a customer as a vendor on the street or in a diner increases it to $1-2 per cup. In 1993, Starbucks partnered with Barnes and Noble bookstores to provide in-house coffee shops, benefiting both retailers and establishing a positive experience for the customer. The cost per cup of coffee is $2-6.

The Four-Stages Economic Progression

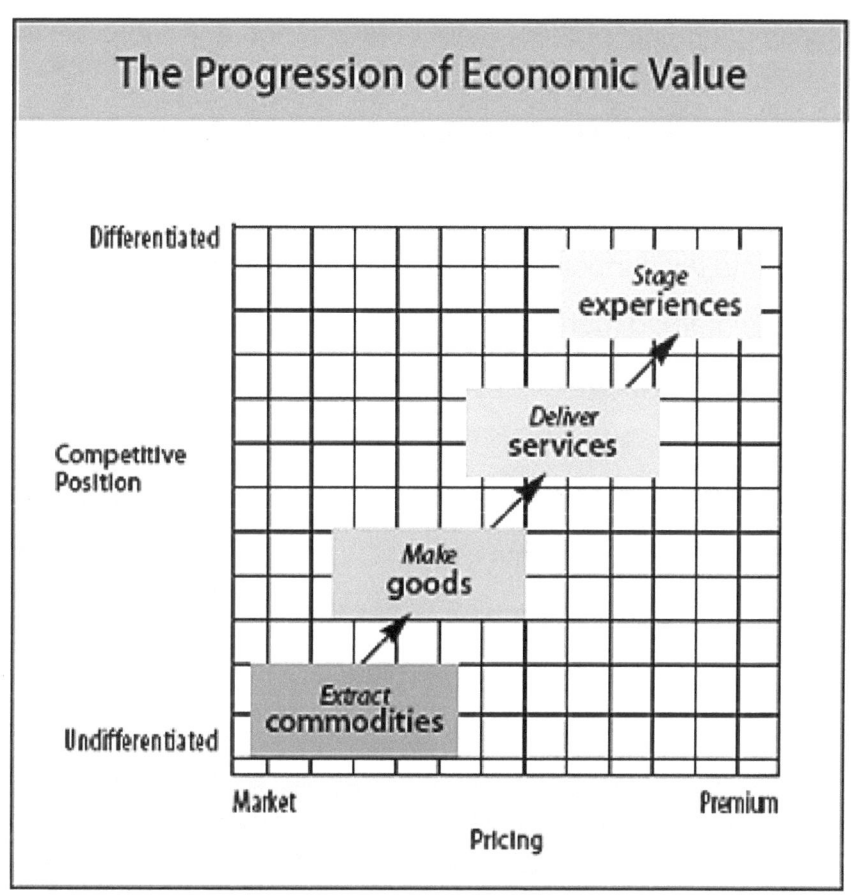

The Evolution of a Child's Birthday Celebration

Let's look at the Four-Stage Economic Progression of a child's birthday celebration. Prior to 1960 mothers made birthday cakes from scratch, mixing farm commodities (flour, sugar, butter, and eggs) that together cost mere dimes. As the goods-based industrial economy advanced, Pillsbury, Duncan Hines and Betty Crocker introduced cake mixes. Mothers began using cake mixes that only required one of two other ingredients to make a cake. Now, birthday cakes went from costing a few cents to costing about $2. In the 80's women were entering the workforce more than ever, and the service economy was taking hold. Moms were too busy to bake a cake. Instead they purchased the birthday cake from a bakery or grocery store costing $10-$15. Now, in the fourth stage of experience economic progression, parents don't have time to bake the cake and or have enough energy to plan and throw the party. So, they "outsource" everything to places like Chuck E. Cheese for $100-$200 or even more. Value is added at each stage making the final product more differentiated and more costly.

Experiences as Values

Experiences are a source of value. Walt Disney made a name for himself by layering experiential effects into his cartoons. Then, in 1955 he opened Disneyland where the customer was now *immersed* (connection and participation) in the cartoon world. About 10 years later he opened Walt Disney World. He pioneered the first *themed* amusement parks.

Retailers rarely develop a theme or think about CXM. Instead they talk about "shopping experiences". They fail to create a theme that ties their merchandise to something the customer admires, wants or needs. But, a few retailers understand CXM. Three of them are Barnes & Noble, Cabela's, and M&Ms.

Just by observation, the CEO of Barnes & Noble noticed that customers walked through his store not only to browse or buy a book, but to *socialize*. They wanted to talk to other people as a part of their experience. He thought that aspect of shopping in his store was so important that he changed the architecture of the building, trained his employees differently in how they interacted with customers, and also added decor and furnishings.

Cabela's created an outdoor theme for customers shopping for hunting and fishing gear. They have taxidermied animals mounted on the wall or in displays throughout the store, backdrops of outdoor scenes, and artificial trees and bushes.

M&M's has created an experience in both their stores and on their website. If you go to their website you can create your own M&M's by choosing colors, images, messages, and the kind of packaging you want. Their store is called M&M's World. Each color of M&M is "characterized". You can buy shirts, candy dispensers, drinkware, and other accessories.

Is it possible for your business to a establish a *theme*? The theme is the foundation and should be closely tied to your brand, while the experiences you stage make an impression. And it is the *impressions* customers take away. Establish cues throughout different areas of your business that support the theme. At Rainforest Cafe', for example, the hostess does not say, "Let me show you to your table." Instead, he or she says, "Your adventure is about to begin." And when you leave, the only way out is through their gift shop (another planned touch point).

More Examples in Different Industries
Consider Las Vegas as the experience capital of the world. Everything is designed to be an experience like the slot machines at the airport as you as you arrive, gambling casinos, themed hotels and restaurants, and the many show options such as music, comedy, the circus, and magic.

Some restaurants have taken experiences and staged them in a way that customers feel like they got more than just a meal. Examples are Hard Rock Cafe', Rainforest Cafe', Bubba Gump Shrimp Co., and Planet Hollywood. It goes beyond just staging an experience for the customer. You must also *engage* (connection and participation) with them. Retail stores such a Niketown, Cabela's, and Bass Pro Shop have added experiences into their stores. And places like Brookstone and the Sharper Image let people play with the gadgets they sell.

Customers and businesses are complex. You might have many product/service lines, and many customer segments to address. Leadership ensures that everyone in your business engages in CXM. A few ideas to get the process started are: 1) conducting surveys, 2) using focus groups, 3) observing customers, 4) and start thinking of your products and services as verbs (what do they *do*?) and how are they involved in developing your CXM plan. For example, manufacturers need to think about the experience customers will have by using their products. It's not about the good, it's about the customer. Consider the manufacturer of golf clubs. The golfer wants to improve their game by using your golf clubs. Think of the golfer, not the clubs.

Goals for Commodity-Based, Goods-Based, & Service-Based Companies
Companies in each stage of the economy need goals based on what they do before setting the stage to establish great CXM. Some of their goals before CXM might be:

Commodities:

       Discover new substances

       Extract materials efficiently

       Explore alternate sites

       Trade in markets

Goods:

       Invent new products

       Make products more efficient

       Improving existing products

       Sell goods to users

Services:

       Develop better procedures

       Deliver operations efficiently

Provide timely responses to customers

Interact with clients

Now, how are your going to create an amazing model and theme for CXM?

Depict Scripts - what employees say at certain times and what they say. An example is the hostess at the Rainforest Cafe' who says, "Your adventure is about to begin."

Stage Event Efficiently - consider sequence, progression, and duration. For example, if you have a Mexican food restaurant with a mariachi band, you need to set the duration of time they play at any one table.

Preserving Memories - you might be able to sell souvenirs, take a free picture with your guests, or sell t-shirts if it is some kind of sporting event. This part mainly depends on the type of business you operate.

Encountering Guests - each employee should stick to their own role or "character" when interacting with guests. This boils down to training, so they can learn their character or role and what they can and cannot do.

The Three Cues of CXM

We know we need to *connect* with the customer and also have the customer *participate* in some kind of experience. There are only three things every business has:

1. The products and/or services they are marketing. For a restaurant it's food.
1) Everything else around it, tangible or intangible, such chairs, tables, plates, silverware, the smell, music, decorations, and other things.

2) People. The employees you hired to perform different job roles and responsibilities.

We are going to refer to these cues as:

1) **Functional Cues**- concern over the quality of the actual product or service you sell. If you are a restaurant, does your food taste good? The Functional Cue is the product or service that your customer is seeking from you. It is the foundation for developing a great experience. Remember that it will be based on perception. And perception is reality. With Functional Cues, be sure to deliver your brand promise and the value propositions that are a part of you image or reputation.

2) **Mechanic Cues** - part of the Mechanic Cue is the environment. Research has shown that the environment alone subconsciously encourages customers to leave or stay. Aside from the atmosphere in your restaurant, other things that serve as mechanic cues include the plates and silverware, tables and tablecloths, music (if any), lighting, cleanliness of the restrooms, among other items. Mechanic Cues are extremely important, because they are part of the experience.

3) **Humanic Cues** - the quality of the interaction between employees and customers. They should all be well trained regarding their roles and their characters. For the restaurant, being greeted at the door by a hostess who takes you to your table, friendliness of the server, efficiency of the server, and perhaps the manager walking past your table to ask if everything is okay. Research shows it is the Humanic Cues that have the deepest connection are remembered longer than the other two cues.The more important, personal, and enduring the customer-service provider interaction is, the more pronounced the effect will be.

Functional, Mechanic, and Humanic Cues tell the whole story of the customer experience. Customization is out of style. Today you need to create *Customer-Unique*

Value. It needs to be specific to the individual customer, particular to its characteristics, and singular in its purpose or value to the customer.

When analyzing the cues you need to work on, identify its category (functional, mechanic, humanic). Then determine if it is a disadvantage or a limitation. A disadvantage is something bad that results by connecting with a certain cue in your business. Perhaps a couple wanted to go on a quiet dinner date and the music and background noise in the restaurant was so loud (disadvantage) they could barely hear each other speak (negative). This is an example of a Mechanic Cue that is a disadvantage. A limitation is a good thing that your business cannot deliver to the customer. For example, assume the same couple went on a date to a quiet restaurant. Everything was nice and quiet about the restaurant, but they don't serve any alcoholic beverages. The couple wanted a bottle of wine (positive thing), but you cannot deliver it to them (limitation). This is a Functional Cue.

The CXM Implementation Process:

List up to 5 Functional Cues and draw a line between each one and the facial expression that you think fits most of your customers' opinions for feelings about it. Be objective and brutally honest.

1)   2)   3)   4)   5)

List up to 5 Mechanic Cues and draw a line between each one and the facial expression that you think fits most of your customers' opinions or feelings about it. Be objective and brutally honest.

1)   2)   3)   4)   5)

List up to 5 Humanic Cues and draw a line between each one and the facial expression that you think fits most of your customers' opinions or feelings about it. Be objective and brutally honest.

1)   2)   3)   4)   5)

Overall, in which cue category does it appear you are doing the best job (Functional, Mechanic, or Humanic)? What do you believe is the main reason for this?

Overall, in which cue category does it appear you are doing in the worst job (Functional, Mechanic, or Humanic? What do you believe is the main reason for this?

Of all the Functional, Mechanic, and Humanic Cues you listed, which three were rated the *lowest*? If more than three have the same rating, select from those to work on three.

Now, Let's Start Taking Your Business to the Next Level Today!

Name the cue that needs improvement and identify the category (Functional, Mechanic, Humanic)_____

Describe it in as much detail as possible:

_____

_____

_____

_____

_____

In your description, circle all of the adjectives or descriptive words used. List those here:

1.

2.

3.

4.

5.

Could be more:

For each descriptor, identify it as positive, neutral, or negative. Of the neutral or negative ones, determine if it is a disadvantage (something that *causes* a negative experience) or if it is a limitation (something that prevents a good experience).

Disadvantages - What can you do to reduce or eliminate this element, so that it does not cause your customer to have a bad experience?

Limitations - What can you do to improve this element or eliminate it, if it is a barrier, so that you customer has a better experience?

Your 2nd Cue to Address:

Name the cue that needs improvement and identify the category (Functional, Mechanic, or

Humanic)_____

Describe it in as much detail as possible:

_____

_____

_____

_____

_____

In your description, circle all of the adjectives or descriptive words used. List those here:

1.

2.

3.

4.

5.

Could be more:

For each descriptor, identify it is positive, neutral or negative. Of the neutral and negative ones, determine if it is a disadvantage (something that *causes* a negative experience) or if it is a limitation (something that prevents a good experience).

Disadvantages - What can you do to reduce or eliminate this element so that it does not cause your customer to have a bad experience?

Limitations - What can you do to improve this element or eliminate it, if it is a barrier, so that you customer has a better experience?

Your 3rd Cue to Address

Name the cue that needs improvement and identify the category (Functional, Mechanic, Humanic)_____

Describe it in as much detail as possible:

_____
_____
_____
_____
_____

In your description, circle all of the adjectives or descriptive words used. List those here:

1.

2.

3.

4.

5.

For each one, identify it is positive, neutral or negative. Of the neutral and negative ones, determine if it is a disadvantage (something that *causes* a negative experience) or if it is a limitation (something that prevents a good experience).

Disadvantages - What can you do to reduce or eliminate this element so that it does not cause your customer to have a bad experience?

Limitations - What can you do to improve this element or eliminate it, if it is a barrier, so that you customer has a better experience?

CXM Goal-Setting

Now that we know what needs to be done to improve your customers' experiences with your business, it is time to set some goals.

Cue 1: _____

Set at least one SMART goal to address it. Specific, Measureable, Attainable, Relevant, and Timebound

_____

_____

_____

_____

Cue 2: _____

Set at least one SMART goal to address it. Specific, Measureable, Attainable, Relevant, and Timebound

_____

_____

_____

_____

Cue 3: _____

Set at least one SMART goal to address it. Specific, Measureable, Attainable, Relevant, and Timebound

_____

_____

_____

_____

Overall Perspective & Conclusions

If you achieved all three goals related to the cues that need improvement, how do you think it will impact your business in 3-months? 6-months? If you practiced using the CXM process at the end of each quarter, how do you think it will impact your business in 1-year? 3-years? 5-years? CXM is essential in today's highly competitive environment due to technology, globalization, and more educated customers. Each customer should feel as though he or she gained a *Customer-Unique Value* by purchasing your products or services. There is more to your business than what you sell. You have to remember that all three cues, Functional, Mechanic, and Humanic are all important. Every "touch point" your customer has from the time he or she begins interaction with your business until the end should be analyzed. Use the CXM Model at the end of every quarter to see how your business is doing.

An example of **Zedric's Restaurant ~ Fit with Flavor** is included below to demonstrate how CXM works throughout an entire business.

Restaurant Example: Zedric's ~ Fit with Flavor

This case focuses on a unique business that is a little hard to classify, but it operates in the restaurant industry. The business is called Zedric's. They make healthy, gourmet food to-go, and their slogan is "Fit with Flavor".

Executive Chef Zach Lutton began his culinary career with Chef Bruce Auden in the Biga on the Banks kitchen, one of the most popular fine dining restaurants in San Antonio, while attending college. He quickly caught the cooking bug. He later cooked for HEB Central Market and worked under Chef Laurel Waters at the Laurel Tree before moving to New York to further his culinary education. Upon graduation from the Culinary Institute of America in Hyde Park, New York, Chef Zach Lutton decided to move back home to San Antonio, Texas to be closer to friends and family. He worked as a Sous Chef at the Dominion, then as an Executive Chef for Compass Group.

What Zach noticed through his experience was that there was a major shortage of healthy, delicious food in San Antonio, and that it was a difficult place to be health conscious. He began cooking healthy meals, at first for himself, and then as a service for friends and other acquaintances on weekends, receiving rave reviews along the way. He was soon bombarded with requests from his relatives, friends, and acquaintances who wanted him to cook for them. They were literally demanding his services. After witnessing the physical transformation of several close friends, he and business partners, brother Vince and their mom Elaine, realized they could potentially provide this city a great
service. They opened Zedric's, to provide a healthy, flavorful and convenient alternative to fast food while still retaining the bold, spicy flavors of South Texas (*Functional Cue*).

Vince Lutton has a degree in Computer Science, with a background in web development with Server Beach, and handles all of Zedric's technology development.

Elaine has an entrepreneurial background, most recently in real estate investment and remodeling. Growing up in a family laden with Physicians, all three owners had strong influences concerning wellness through healthy eating and exercise.

Zedric's is not your traditional restaurant. It is more service-oriented, providing healthy gourmet food to a market that is in need of Chef Zach's talents and products (*Functional Cue*). The prices are very moderate, with most lunch and dinner entrees under $10.00 and breakfast items under $7.00 (*Mechanic Cue*).

When you walk into Zedric's, you are greeted with a smile and an offer of help from a friendly employee (*Humanic Cue*). You might be there for one of three reasons: 1) to select a dish from the well-stocked refrigerator (*Mechanic Cue*) to heat up and eat there. They have enough tables for about 20 people; 2) to select one or two entrées from the refrigerator to take home and eat; or 3) to pick up your preorder -- an entire week's worth of food that is bagged up and ready for you when you arrive. The restaurant interior has a very modern clean appearance, and everything is in their signature colors of orange and white (*Mechanic Cue*).

All the ingredients Chef Zach uses are fresh and healthy, many of them coming from local suppliers such as Peeler Farms, who have pasteurized chickens instead of caged chickens. Peeler is also one of the suppliers in the area of grass-fed beef and lamb. He not only makes good use of the farmer's markets to buy meat, but to select in-season fruits and vegetables along with other items such as herbs, eggs, fruits, honey, granola, and fresh goat cheeses (*Functional Cue*). Chef Zach's menu items change frequently, not only to factor in the season, but also to provide customers variety to keep them coming back (*Mechanic Cue*).

Each dish comes in two sizes: regular and large. This allows the customer to control their caloric intake (*Mechanic Cue*). The meal comes in a tightly sealed plastic dish that can be heated in the microwave. A sticker is wrapped around the dish to ensure it has not been opened. That sticker not only tells you the name of the dish, but all the nutritional facts such as calories, fat grams, protein grams, carbohydrate grams, and sodium. It also informs you on the vitamins and minerals in each dish (*Mechanic Cue*).

You can walk into Zedric's and look through the glass of the refrigerator to see what is available. As mentioned earlier, you can either select something and eat it there or take it home. Some patrons use Zedric's to provide their meals for the entire week: breakfast, lunch, and dinner. They can come in and make all of their selections there; or they can order online (*Mechanic Cue*), where they select all their meals, choose a pick-up day and window of time, and then stop by to receive their order. When the customer arrives, all the meals are bagged up and ready to take home (*Mechanic Cue*). If you are a regular and they see your car pulling in, they will go get your order and have it waiting at the front desk as you enter the front door and greet you by name (*Humanic Cue*).

All Zedric's foods are good for seven days, except fish dishes, which should be consumed in five days. All labels have an expiration date (*Functional Cue*). Even during the online ordering process, you can see all the nutritional information (*Mechanic Cue*). An example of a dinner entrées is *Beef Tenderloin with Sweet Potato Hash*: marinated and grilled beef tenderloin with a side of sweet potato hash, topped with Zedric's own chermoula sauce.

A breakfast entrée example is *Scrambled Eggs & Home Fries*: Organic, pasture-raised eggs served with crisp homestyle new potatoes with sautéed onions, poblanoes, and red peppers topped with their housemade serrano catsup (*Functional Cue*). Zedric's also carries a wine selection from Texas wineries (*Mechanic Cue*). The employees can help you select wines that pair well with the meals you selected (*Humanic Cue*).

Zedric's employees are very customer-centric. One example of this is when a regular customer arrived to pick up her meals for the week, they were out of one of the selections she had made, so the co-owner Elaine, allowed her to select another entrée to replace it even if it cost more and then she gave her an extra entrée for the inconvenience. Both meals were free (*Humanic Cue*).

Chef Zach knows the importance of certain diet trends. On his menu, he has a special sign to indicate if the meal is vegetarian, low calorie, gluten free, low in carbohydrates, or Paleo (*Mechanic Cue*). This helps customers select dishes with more than just the nutritional information provided on the product itself. Zedric's also has a registered dietician who will sit down with you for free and help you select the right meals and the right size of those meals (*Humanic Cue*).

Chef Zach also caters weddings, business functions, or whatever event the customer may need. This family of entrepreneurs found a great opportunity in the marketplace, but more importantly, they understand how to operate a business by placing the functional, mechanic, and humanic clues at the forefront of all that they do. As a result, they are growing: they just opened a second location, and has started offering delivery service (*Mechanic Cue*).

REFERENCES

OTHER RESOURCES AND TOOLS